TESTING AND ASSESSMENT IN THE NATIO

Pupils between the ages of 7 and 11 (Years 3–6) cover Key S
Curriculum. In May of their final year of Key Stage 2 (Year 6), all pupils take written
National Tests (commonly known as SATs) in the three core subjects: English, Maths
and Science. Your child should already have taken some National Tests at the end
of Key Stage 1 (Year 2) in Maths (number, shape and space), English Reading and
English Writing.

At the end of Key Stage 1, children are awarded a National Curriculum level for each
subject tested. When children eventually take Key Stage 2 tests, they are again awarded
a level. On average, pupils are expected to advance one level for every two years they
are at school. The target for pupils at the end of Key Stage 1 is Level 2. By the end of
Key Stage 2, four years later, the target is Level 4. The table below shows the average
target levels.

		7 years	**11 years**
---	---	:---::	:---:
▢ Exceptional performance	Level 6		▢
	Level 5		▢
▢ Exceeded targets for age group	Level 4	▢	▢
▢ Achieved targets for age group	Level 3	▢	▢
	Level 2	▢	▢
▢ Working towards targets for age group	Level 1	▢	▢

IMPROVING YOUR CHILD'S UNDERSTANDING AT KEY STAGE 2

This series will help you to work with your child to improve his or her knowledge and
understanding of English, Maths and Science throughout Key Stage 2. There are four
books for each subject – one for each year, starting with 7–8 year-olds. The activities in
the books are appropriate to the target levels for each year and to the topics your child
will study during that year.

These books may be used in conjunction with Letts' Progress Test books, also in the
At Home With The National Curriculum range. The books provide test materials to assess
your child's level of knowledge at each year of Key Stage 2 and so tell you the areas in
which he or she needs most help.

HELPING YOUR CHILD TO LEARN

HOW TO USE THIS BOOK

The work in this book covers Levels 4–5 and is appropriate for the average 10–11 year-old. This book contains the following features:

Thirteen four-page Units (pages 3–54) each incorporating:

- Notes to parents, explaining the relevance of the topic to the National Curriculum, a description of the activity and helpful 'Teaching points' advising you how to tackle common areas of difficulty.
- Two colourful information and activity pages for your child to work through with your help or on his or her own.
- Further questions and activities related to the topic, accompanied by more ideas for helping your child to understand the subject.

The topics covered in this book, and their page numbers, are as follows:

Answers are provided at the back of the book.

Working through this book with your child

- Your child should not attempt to do all the activities in the book in one go. Work through each topic Unit together, allowing plenty of time for discussion and explanation of the subject. Encourage your child to attempt as many of the activities as possible without help, then use the further activities and ideas to expand on the subject. Do not move on to the next Unit until your child fully understands the one he or she is working on.
- When your child has completed one activity spread, turn to the Answers section at the back of the book. Check the answers with your child and discuss why they are right or wrong.
- If your child has difficulty understanding a particular topic, the 'More ways to help your child' section offers methods of explaining a subject in less formal situations. Most of these may be adapted for use during everyday activities such as shopping or cooking.

Equipment your child will need

The following may be needed for answering the questions in this book:

- a pen or pencil for writing, a pencil for drawing, a rubber and coloured pencils;
- a ruler (30cm plastic ruler is most suitable);
- a calculator;
- spare paper.

Individual topic Units might require additional simple equipment. Make sure you have everything ready before beginning each Unit.

Here comes the post

Introduction:

Earlier books in this series developed work on addition and subtraction, beginning with mental activities involving simple number bonds to 10, then to 20 and later to 100. This was followed by work on the vertical written method, used in school for numbers too large to work with mentally. In the case of subtraction, this involved the popular **decomposition** method where the tens number is 'broken down' to help out the units number in cases when a straightforward subtraction is difficult, such as 54 – 29.

It is important, of course, for children to be confident in their ability to handle addition and subtraction questions. Of equal importance, however, is the ability to use and apply these skills to real-life situations (when shopping, reading timetables, following recipes etc.). To help children to use their skills outside maths lessons, it is necessary to place them in situations that call for more than just the answer to a laid out 'sum'. For example, they need to be able to make decisions about not just *how* to do a question but *what* to do, in other words, do they add, subtract, multiply or divide?

National Curriculum:

Attainment Target 2: Number and Algebra

The National Curriculum at Key Stage 2 expects children to use and apply mathematics in practical tasks, in real-life problems and in mathematics itself. At Key Stage 2 children are expected to:

*choose methods of computation appropriate to a problem,
adapt them and apply them accurately.*

Level 4 expects children to be developing their own strategies for solving problems. At Level 5 children must have developed this further, including being able to identify and obtain necessary information from a problem situation, and check their results to decide whether they are sensible.

Activity:

The activities in this Unit are concerned with helping children to develop the ability to use and apply their skills in addition and subtraction. As such, it also addresses Attainment Target 1: Using and Applying Mathematics. Children need to face situations in which decisions must be made about what to do. The skills it is important for children to develop include the ability to decide what maths is needed in a particular situation, to decide what information is relevant to the question, and to organise this information effectively towards solving the problem.

Teaching points:

Focus on what needs to be done to solve a mathematical problem rather than on just how to do it. For example, a distance sign passed on the motorway says 'Reading 39 miles, Windsor 19 miles'. How do we find the distance **between** the two towns? In this case, of course, we subtract, but many children who could readily find the answer to $\frac{39}{-19}$ have difficulty in deciding what type of calculation to do.

3

Here comes the post

Sue works extremely hard delivering the post to people living in four different towns.

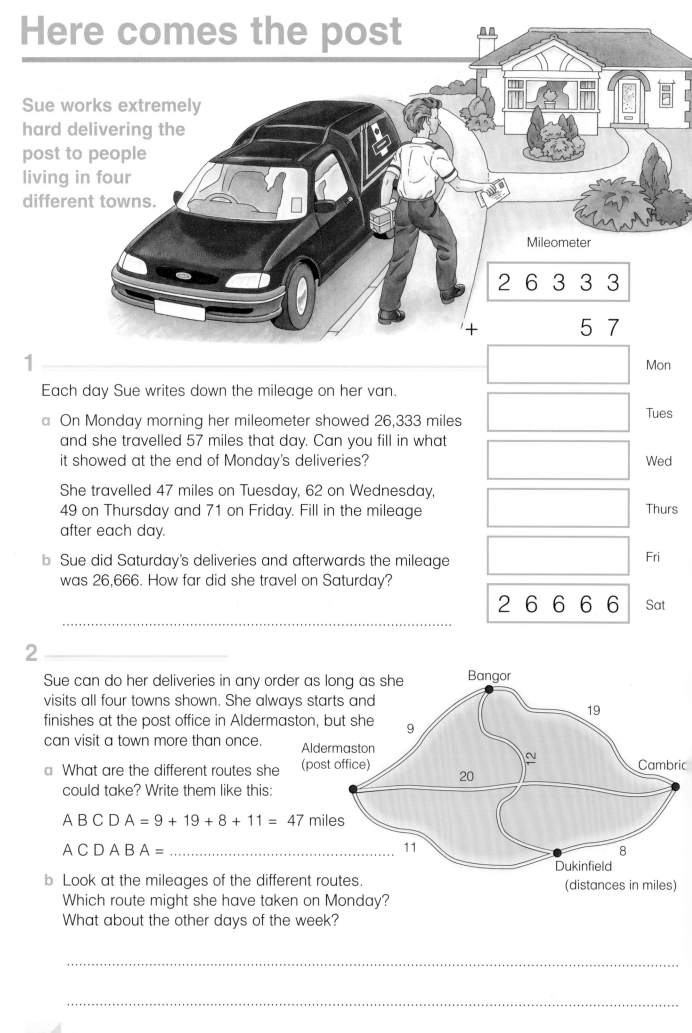

Mileometer

| 2 6 3 3 3 |

+ 5 7

| | Mon
| | Tues
| | Wed
| | Thurs
| | Fri
| 2 6 6 6 6 | Sat

1

Each day Sue writes down the mileage on her van.

a On Monday morning her mileometer showed 26,333 miles and she travelled 57 miles that day. Can you fill in what it showed at the end of Monday's deliveries?

She travelled 47 miles on Tuesday, 62 on Wednesday, 49 on Thursday and 71 on Friday. Fill in the mileage after each day.

b Sue did Saturday's deliveries and afterwards the mileage was 26,666. How far did she travel on Saturday?

....

2

Sue can do her deliveries in any order as long as she visits all four towns shown. She always starts and finishes at the post office in Aldermaston, but she can visit a town more than once.

a What are the different routes she could take? Write them like this:

A B C D A = 9 + 19 + 8 + 11 = 47 miles

A C D A B A = ...

b Look at the mileages of the different routes. Which route might she have taken on Monday? What about the other days of the week?

....

....

Bangor

19

9

Aldermaston (post office)

20

12

Cambric

11

8

Dukinfield (distances in miles)

4

3

On Saturday, after her deliveries, Sue stops at Ashbury's Supermarket. As she puts things in her trolley, she jots down how much they cost to roughly work out the bill. When she has all her items she pairs or groups them, like this:

- The cheese costing £1.21 she puts with the 80p carton of milk.
- The cat food costing 62p goes with the apples at £1.44.
- Three 32p bags of crisps can be grouped together.
- The frozen pizza at £4.99 stays on its own.

Can you see what she is doing? She is putting together items that roughly make one pound, or two pounds, or three pounds and so on.

Her bill will come to roughly £10.00.
Check with a calculator to see if she is about right.

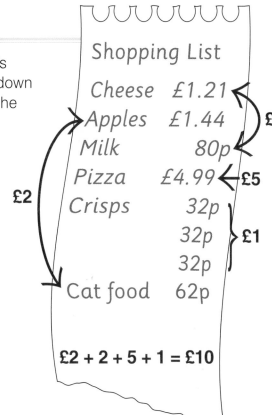

Shopping List

Cheese	£1.21
Apples	£1.44
Milk	80p
Pizza	£4.99
Crisps	32p
	32p
	32p
Cat food	62p

£2 + 2 + 5 + 1 = £10

a

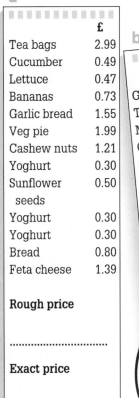

	£
Tea bags	2.99
Cucumber	0.49
Lettuce	0.47
Bananas	0.73
Garlic bread	1.55
Veg pie	1.99
Cashew nuts	1.21
Yoghurt	0.30
Sunflower seeds	0.50
Yoghurt	0.30
Yoghurt	0.30
Bread	0.80
Feta cheese	1.39

Rough price

....

Exact price

....

b

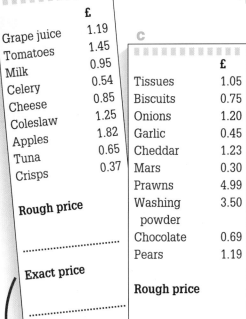

	£
Grape juice	1.19
Tomatoes	1.45
Milk	0.95
Celery	0.54
Cheese	0.85
Coleslaw	1.25
Apples	1.82
Tuna	0.65
Crisps	0.37

Rough price

....

Exact price

....

Difference = ...

c

	£
Tissues	1.05
Biscuits	0.75
Onions	1.20
Garlic	0.45
Cheddar	1.23
Mars	0.30
Prawns	4.99
Washing powder	3.50
Chocolate	0.69
Pears	1.19

Rough price

....

Exact price

....

Difference = ...

4

Try adding the bills opposite in the same way by grouping prices together. Remember:

10 + 90 = 100	5 + 95 = 100
20 + 80 = 100	15 + 85 = 100
30 + 70 = 100	25 + 75 = 100
40 + 60 = 100	35 + 65 = 100
50 + 50 = 100	45 + 55 = 100

Fill in the rough price on the bills and then, using a calculator (or adding the numbers on paper), find the exact price.

Now fill in the difference in price between the rough and exact totals.

rence = ...

Now turn over ➤

5

Now try these ...

1 The table shows routes on the map. Work out how far each route is in your head. Can you find some more routes to work out?

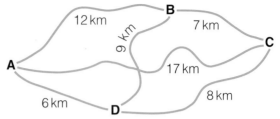

Starting and finishing at A		Starting and finishing at B	
From A to A	**Distance**	**From B to B**	**Distance**
ABCA		BCDB	
ADBA		BADB	
ABCDA		BDCAB	
ACBDA		BCADB	
ADBCA		BACDB	
ABDCA		BDACB	

2 Read these mileometers to find how far has been travelled.

Before	54542	Before	34671	Before	26482	Before	76234
After	54653	After	35624	After	27115	After	79103

Distance ....   Distance ....   Distance ....   Distance ....

Before	33443	Before	71849	Before	63829	Before	33856
After	41126	After	88100	After	72000	After	40000

Distance ....   Distance ....   Distance ....   Distance ....

3 Add these shopping bills roughly, then exactly.

£1.59	£2.40	£0.23	£1.49	£2.25
£1.34	£0.81	£4.10	£3.08	£1.10
£0.40	£2.85	£1.02	£2.60	£1.99
£2.99	£0.18	£4.09	£0.55	£0.89
£1.05	£0.99	£2.19	£5.10	£0.36

rough total ....   rough ....   rough ....   rough ....   rough ....

exact total ....   exact ....   exact ....   exact ....   exact ....

More ways to help your child:

Practise adding numbers mentally when shopping, with door numbers, passing buses etc.

Help your child's dexterity with numbers with the 'faulty key' activity. On a calculator, imagine certain keys don't work, for example the 6 and 9. Can you find the answers to the following calculations on the calculator avoiding the broken keys: 6 + 6, 6 + 9, 9 + 16, 26 + 16, 6 × 6, 29 × 16.

Prime suspect

Introduction:

Multiplication is usually introduced to children as being repeated addition (where 9 + 9 + 9 can be thought of as 3 × 9, expressed as 3 times 9, or 3 lots of 9) – as a shorthand method of adding. To use this shorthand, children must know their tables. The focus of this Unit is to put tables to good use in developing the skills of written multiplication.

It is important for children to extend their knowledge of the language associated with multiplication, and this Unit introduces the following terms: **multiple** – a number created by multiplying two numbers together (so 12 is a multiple of 3 and 4, and also of 6 and 2, and 12 and 1); **factor** – a number that divides evenly into another number (so the factors of 12 are 12, 6, 4, 3, 2 and 1); **prime number** – a number which has only two factors, itself and 1, for example 3, 11, 17; **square number** – created by multiplying a number by itself, for example 1 (1 × 1), 4 (2 × 2), 9, 16 and 100.

National Curriculum:

Attainment Target 2: Number and Algebra

The National Curriculum expects children to learn their tables and to be able to use written methods of multiplication. At Key Stage 2 it states that children should:

know the multiplication facts to 10 × 10,
and use a range of mental and written methods.

Level 4 requires children to know all the tables to 10 × 10 and to know how to do multiplication on paper. Level 5 expects children to be able to multiply a three-digit number by a two-digit number without a calculator.

Activity:

Many ideas to help children learn their tables were introduced in Books 1, 2 and 3. These are briefly revisited to complete all the tables facts to 10 × 10. Further activities introduce the terms square number, rectangular number, factor, multiple and prime number. Later activities focus on the written method of multiplication children are likely to meet in school, and this extends to three-digit by two-digit questions (such as 485 × 35). The emphasis is on children understanding what is happening when they use a particular method and why it works.

Teaching points:

Test your child on his or her table facts as individual facts rather than as a sequence, for example 4 × 9 = 36, 7 × 4 = 28, rather than 'one three is three, two threes are ...' etc.

Provide squared paper for your child to investigate which numbers are rectangular and which are prime. (A **rectangular** number is defined as a number that can be drawn as a rectangle with more than one row or column, for example 6 is a rectangular number ▦ .)

When your child is performing long multiplication, encourage him or her initially to draw a rectangle in the way shown, to illustrate the stages involved. This emphasises place value ideas and is important in ensuring your child understands and remembers the shortened version commonly used.

Prime suspect

Here is a quick way of making a tables square. For this you'll need to copy and cut out the L shape from page 55.

1

By putting your L shape on the squared paper you can make rectangles of different sizes. The blue edges of the grid and the L shape make the borders of a rectangle. Count the number of squares in the rectangle (the area) and write that number in the bottom right hand square, like the 20 shown opposite. Do this for all the rectangles on the grid below until every square has a number in it. Some have been done for you.

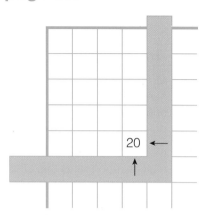

What do you notice about the numbers?

....

The answer to a table fact can be found by making a rectangle and counting the number of squares. The numbers 1, 4, 9, 16 ... (going diagonally) are called **square numbers**. Can you see why? Which other numbers are square numbers?

....

2

The rectangles opposite show different tables facts, all with the answer 12. The first rectangle has sides of 3 and 4, and has 12 squares.

3 and **4** are **factors** of **12**.
2 and **6** are factors of 12.
1 and **12** are also factors of 12.

All the factors of 12 are 1, 2, 3, 4, 6 and 12. 12 is also known as a **multiple** of 1, 2, 3, 4, 6 and 12.

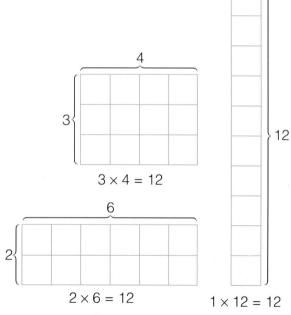

What are all the factors of 8?
(Try drawing different rectangles with 8 squares.)

....

3

Using the squared paper opposite, draw a rectangle with 7 squares. The only rectangle you will be able to make is a 1 × 7 rectangle. That means that the number 7 only has two factors, 1 and 7! Any number that has only two factors (itself and 1) is known as a **prime** number. A number which isn't prime is known as a **rectangular** number.

Try to draw rectangles with more than one row or column for each of the numbers below. Write the list of factors underneath and whether they are prime or rectangular numbers. The first one has been done for you.

6	13	9	5

3 × 2
6 × 1
Rectangular

4

In Book 3 we multiplied numbers such as **538 × 9** by splitting the number up and multiplying each part at a time.

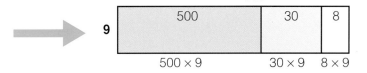

With harder numbers such as: 5 2
                                 × 6 4

we can draw a rectangle to help us. We multiply each part and then add them together:

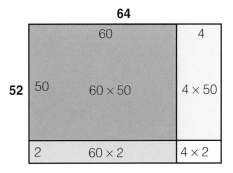

```
      5 2
    × 6 4
        8   (4 × 2)
    2 0 0   (4 × 50)
    1 2 0   (60 × 2)
  + 3 0 0 0 (60 × 50)
    3 3 2 8
```

(3328 is a **multiple** of 52 and 64)

With larger numbers, such as **162 × 23** we can also split the numbers like this: Can you work out the answers?

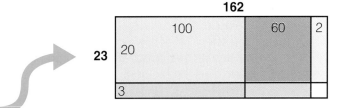

Now turn over ➤

9

Now try these ...

1   Draw a **square** around any square numbers and draw a **circle** around any prime numbers you can see.

12		3		14		1		18		2

      5   64   9   15   3   16

8   7   49   21   13   39

      4   164   99   81   12   71

2   List all the factors of these numbers.

24 ....   29 ....

18 ....   30 ....

36 ....   51 ....

48 ....   64 ....

3   Can you do these?

24	32	39	43	156	384
× 16	× 15	× 23	× 34	× 39	× 61

What's left?

Introduction:

There are many ways of approaching a division question such as $16\overline{\smash{)}832}$. One way of solving it is without using division at all. We can turn it into a multiplication question by asking, 'How many lots of 16 make 832?' It is important for children to see the relationship between multiplication and division – each is the inverse, or opposite, of the other: $832 \div 16 = 52$, so $52 \times 16 = 832$. This relationship can help us to check answers to division questions by multiplying and vice versa. The method a child uses to solve division questions is of no importance in itself; what matters is that it is an efficient way of working which consistently produces right answers and which the child understands. The work in Books 2 and 3 was concerned with helping children to make sense of division. A written method of division was introduced, which built on children's early sharing experiences in school. This method is developed in this Unit, to deal with more sophisticated division questions, including those which require a decimal answer.

National Curriculum:

Attainment Target 2: Number and Algebra

At Key Stage 2, the National Curriculum expects children to develop methods of division:

for up to three-digit by two-digit numbers and with decimals.

Knowledge of multiplication tables is a great help when doing division. Level 4 requires all tables up to 10×10 to have been mastered. Level 4 also expects children to be able to divide whole numbers by 10 and 100. Level 5 extends this to include division by 1000, division with decimals to two places, and division of any three-digit number by any two-digit number.

Activity:

The activities in this Unit begin with some revision of work covered in Book 3 which looked at division questions involving remainders. The early method of division, which leaves remainders untouched as in '16 remainder 8', is developed to show children how the remainders themselves can be divided up. This involves the introduction of division with decimals to allow 16 remainder 8 to be recorded as 16.5.

While it is important for children to be able to deal with remainders in this way, it is also necessary for them to think about the context in which the division is set, because it is not always appropriate to divide up the remainder and include it in the answer. For example, the answer to 'How many 26p stamps can I buy for £2.00?' is 7 and not 7.692. Children need plenty of practice with division questions in a variety of contexts if they are to develop a 'sense' of division. Throughout all the books in this series, the relationship between division and multiplication has been stressed and there is more advanced work in this Unit to develop the link further.

Teaching points:

Encourage your child to draw out questions to help visualise the role of the remainder, for example 66 people travelling 8 to a car, will need 9 cars; while 66p used to buy 8p sweets will only purchase 8 sweets, leaving 2p remaining. Diagrams can assist your child in making decisions about remainders in real-life division problems.

What's left?

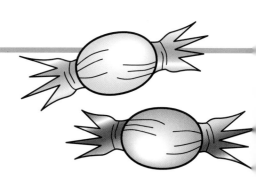

Division is about sharing things fairly.
Sometimes numbers do not divide exactly so we
have to decide what to do with any **remainders**.

1

Look at this division question: **18 ÷ 4**.
Share out 4 each and you are left with
remainder 2.

We can simply leave the answer with
a remainder

    as $18 \div 4 = $ **4 r 2**

or we can go further, and share the remainder,
by splitting it into parts (such as a decimal
or a fraction).

Take the remainder 2 and split it into 4 parts.

Making $4\frac{1}{2}$ or 4.5 your answer.

    $18 \div 4 = $ **4.5**

$$18 \div 4$$

  4   4   4   4   r2

$4\frac{1}{2}$ $4\frac{1}{2}$ $4\frac{1}{2}$ $4\frac{1}{2}$

2

It is important to learn how to divide and give an answer with decimals,
rather than just remainders. Here's how to do it!

(You will need to remember: 1 unit = 10 tenths, 2 units = 20 tenths and so on.)

	$4\overline{)58}$	58 to be shared between 4,
4 x **10**	-40	10 to each uses 40.
	1 8 left	18 to be shared between 4,
4 x **4**	-16	4 to each uses 16.
	2 left	2 units (20 tenths) shared between 4,
4 x **0.5**	$-$ 2.0	5 tenths each uses 20 tenths (2 units).

So the answer to 58 ÷ 4 = **14.5**.

Try these in the same way:

52 ÷ 8 =   **154 ÷ 5 =**   **462 ÷ 5 =**

3

Sometimes, however, giving an answer as a decimal doesn't make sense.

Listen to this.

There are 28 children to be shared out among 8 cars. This means there will be **3.5** children in each car!

So, when you are answering a question, make sure the answer you give makes sense!

4

If I had £2.00 how many 26p stamps could I buy?

1 stamp	26p
2 stamps	52p
3 stamps	78p
4 stamps	104p
5 stamps	130p
6 stamps	156p
7 stamps	182p
8 stamps	208p

← £2.00

On a calculator the answer to 2.00 ÷ 0.26 would come out as 7.6923076 which doesn't make sense! This means 7 whole stamps and 0.6923076 parts of a stamp!

Since you can't buy part of a 26p stamp like this, the answer is 7 stamps and you'll have some change left.

To find out how much change, work out 7 lots of 26p = £1.82 and subtract this from your original amount of money.

5

Now try answering these.

a How many 26p stamps can I buy with £2.50? ....

b If I had £2.00 how many bags of crisps could I buy at 28p each? ....

c If I had £2.00 how many bars of chocolate could I buy at 35p each? ....

d If I had £10.00 how many magazines could I buy at 75p each? ....

How much change you will have for each one?

a .... b .... c .... d ....

Now turn over ➤

Now try these ...

1   a   How many cars that seat 5 people will be needed to take 29 children
on a school trip? (Remember that each car needs an adult driving it.)   ....

   b   How many egg boxes will I need to store 43 eggs? (There are
6 eggs in each box.)   ....

   c   What number of 8 seater mini-buses will I need to take 94 people
on an outing?   ....

2   How many 26p stamps can I buy with (use a calculator to help):

£2.60 ....   £2.86 ....   £2.85 ....   £3.11 ....   £3.00 ....

£4.20 ....   £3.96 ....   £4.68 ....   £5.00 ....   £8.64 ....

3   Work these out, giving a decimal remainder in your answer.

$5\overline{)642}$ $5\overline{)849}$ $4\overline{)546}$ $8\overline{)346}$ $6\overline{)381}$

4   Rewrite these table facts like this:

$6 \times 8 = 48$ $48 \div 6 = 8$ $8 \times 6 = 48$ $48 \div 8 = 6$

$80 \times 7 = 560$ ....

$8 \times 90 =$ ....

$90 \times 60 =$ ....

$70 \times 90 =$ ....

More ways to help your child:

Encourage your child to see division as the opposite of multiplication, so division questions
can be checked using multiplication, for example $432 \div 6 = 72$ can be verified by $6 \times 72 = 432$.

When practising tables, encourage your child to answer questions in reverse, i.e. $9 \times 7 = 63$
becomes $63 \div 7 = 9$ or $63 \div 9 = 7$.

Sharing hard times

Introduction:

The multiplication work in previous books has been concerned with helping children to learn their tables, and to use those tables in mental work and in written multiplication questions. This knowledge of tables facts has also been used in work on division. Children were introduced to a written method of division that helped them to make sense of the process and allowed them to work with tables facts that were familiar. However, there are other skills children need to develop if all this work on multiplication and division is to be really useful to them. Of equal importance is the ability to use and apply these skills of multiplication and division to real-life situations. For example, children need to be able to make use of their mathematics when shopping, reading timetables or working out how long to go before their favourite TV programme. To help children use their skills outside maths lessons, it is necessary to place them in situations that call for more than just the answer to a laid out 'sum'. These skills include the ability to decide what maths is needed in a particular situation, to decide what information is relevant to the question and to organise this information effectively.

National Curriculum:

Attainment Target 2: Number and Algebra

The National Curriculum states that children should use and apply mathematics in practical tasks, in real-life problems and in mathematics itself. At Key Stage 2 children are expected to:

*choose methods of computation appropriate to a problem,
adapt them and apply them accurately.*

Level 4 expects children to be developing their own strategies for solving problems. At Level 5 children must have developed this further, including being able to identify and obtain necessary information from a problem situation and to check their results to decide whether they are sensible.

Activity:

The activities in this Unit are concerned with helping children to develop the ability to use and apply their skills in multiplication and division. As such, it addresses Attainment Target 1: Using and Applying Mathematics, as well as looking at multiplication and division. Children need to face situations in which there are decisions to be made about what to do and whether the answer arrived at is sensible (see 'Teaching points' below).

Teaching points:

Focus on what needs to be done to solve a mathematical problem rather than on just how to do it. For example, if 328 children are going by coach on a school outing, and each coach can take 32 children, how many coaches need to be booked? The need to think about the problem, rather than just dividing 328 by 32 and writing the result, is vital. In the real-life context of coaches, what does 10.25 mean? ($328 \div 32 = 10.25$) Your child needs to think about the answer in the context of the question – the answer is, of course, that 11 coaches are needed.

Do not teach the quick rule 'to multiply by ten add a nought', because with money and decimals this rule does not work and can often produce very inappropriate answers, such as £7.70 × 10 = £7.700. Multiplication by ten involves figures moving one column to the left and division by ten involves moving one column to the right.

Sharing hard times

It's Sophie and Laura's birthday. They are off to Ben's Diner with some friends.

1

Look at the price list. What is the most expensive thing you can buy? What is the cheapest? Which things would you choose? How much would your choice cost?

If you're working out how much your food will cost it is sometimes useful to 'round' the numbers up or down, like this:
instead of two Big Bens at £1.99,
imagine it's two Big Bens at £2 each
and then take away two lots of 1p at the end!
2 × £2 = £4 £4 − 2p = £3.98

Big Ben		**£1.99**
Burger		**79p**
Fries	large	**88p**
	medium	**74p**
	regular	**67p**
Cola		**92p**

If you only had £2.50 to buy something to eat and drink, what could you buy? Write down some combinations on another piece of paper.

2

Sophie and Laura have invited four friends each to Ben's Diner.

How many children are there, including the two girls? ....

If the children all wanted a Big Ben
how much would that cost?   ....
(You could say 10 × £2 and then take
away ten lots of 1p at the end.)

How much would ten milk shakes cost?   ....

What about ten large fries?   ....

A Smiley Meal contains a Big Ben, a milk shake and large fries. It costs £3.98.

How much cheaper is it to buy the Smiley
Meal than buying each part separately?   ....

How much would ten Smiley Meals cost?   ....

Have you noticed what happens when you multiply a number by ten?

Ben's Diner prices are the best!

Milk shake	£1.15
Smiley Meal	£3.98
Apple pie	78p
Ice-cream sundae	£1.25
Coffee	55p
Milk	45p

3

Answer these questions as quickly as possible.

Ten apple pies cost ....   Ten milks cost ....

Ten colas cost ....   Ten regular fries cost ....

How many ice-cream sundaes were bought for £12.50? ....

How many medium fries were bought for £7.40? ....

4

Moving numbers!

Using a calculator, see what happens when you multiply the numbers in the table by ten.

Can you work out any without using a calculator? What do you notice? As each digit becomes ten times bigger they appear to move!

For example: two units becomes 10 × 2 units = 20 units = 2 tens and the 2 moves over into the tens column and so on.

Try multiplying them by 100. How many places do the digits move and in which direction?

See what happens to these numbers when you divide by ten.

What about when you divide by 100?

h	t	u	$\frac{1}{10}$	$\frac{1}{100}$
	2	3	4	5
		4	3	
1	3	8	9	
		9	9	5
		3	0	3
1	0	0	0	1
		0	5	0

Now turn over ➤

Now try these ...

1 Here is the list of things for sale in Carol's Cosy Café.

Carol's Cosy Café			
Price List			
Coffee	70p	Scone	£1.20
Tea	50p	Scone and Jam	£1.55
Cocoa	65p	Teacake	90p
Cola	40p	Toast (1 piece)	85p

How much would these cost?

a 3 coffees and 2 teas   ....

b 2 coffees, 3 cocoas and 4 colas   ....

c 5 teas and 3 scones with jam   ....

d 3 teas and 5 colas   ....

e 4 colas, 5 coffees and 2 teacakes   ....

f 6 pieces of toast, 7 teas and 4 scones ....

Imagine you were really hungry and thirsty.
How much would it cost to buy three of everything? ....

If you were in the café, what would you buy? How much would it cost? ....

What would you buy if you had £5? List different snacks you could have.

....

....

....

2 Answer these questions as quickly as you can. How much does each person get?

a £69 shared between
   ten people   ....

b £4528 shared between
   ten people   ....

c Jeremy won £10
   fourteen times   ....

d Jenny won £75 ten times   ....

e £742 shared between
   a hundred people   ....

f £643,000 shared between
   ten people   ....

g Ian won £1000 three times ....

h Pauline won £125 eight times ....

More ways to help your child:

Using cards with the digits 1 to 9 on, and a counter to represent the decimal point, ask your child to select three number cards and the decimal point and arrange them to make a number smaller than 10. Ask your child to multiply or divide that number by 10 or 100 and encourage him or her to move the cards rather than the counter.

When helping your child to total prices on a calculator, discuss the effect of zeros being omitted. For example, 2.7 should really be £2.70 when dealing with money.

Following the cent

Introduction:

Percentages are closely linked to fractions. Any percentage is simply a fraction whose denominator is 100, so 45% is the same as $\frac{45}{100}$. Percentages are also linked to decimals, where 0.45 means 45 hundredths which in turn means 45%. So fractions, decimals and percentages are simply different ways of expressing a number or amount.

The idea of percentages is an important one because it allows us to make clear comparisons. For example, which of the two test marks, 9 out of 15 or 42 out of 70, is higher? In fact both are 60%. Until we express them as percentages, however, they are difficult to compare. All we are doing is saying, 'If there had been a hundred questions in the test, how many would I have got right at the rate of 9 out of 15, and then at the rate of 42 out of 70?' Percentages, then, simply change fractions, 9 out of 15 or 42 out of 70, to an amount out of a hundred, which allows us to make comparisons much more easily.

National Curriculum:

Attainment Target 2: Number and Algebra

Key Stage 2 requires children to:

understand and use percentages in context,
to estimate, describe and compare proportions of a whole,
and also to calculate percentages of quantities.

Level 4 requires children to use percentages to describe proportions of a whole. Level 5 expects children to calculate percentage parts of quantities (such as in the test results described in the Introduction above).

Activity:

The first activity in this Unit considers simple percentages in the context of a patchwork quilt and, in doing so, revises the notation of percentages (i.e. %) introduced in Book 3. Percentages of quantities such as 200 are then explored, and simple fractions are used to consolidate the link between fractions and percentages, as in 50% = $\frac{1}{2}$, 30% = $\frac{3}{10}$. The activities explain that $\frac{32}{100}$ means 32 ÷ 100 and $\frac{9}{15}$ = 9 ÷ 15. Finally, children are asked to consider a series of test results, convert them to percentages and compare them.

Teaching points:

Your child will find percentages easier if the link with fractions or decimals is emphasised.

Following the cent

This is a picture of part of Mrs Martin's patchwork quilt.

1

How many patches
are there altogether? ....

How many are red? ....

How many are blue? ....

How many are pink? ....

Without counting
can you say how
many are purple? ....

Do you remember the words 'per cent',
which mean 'out of a 100'?

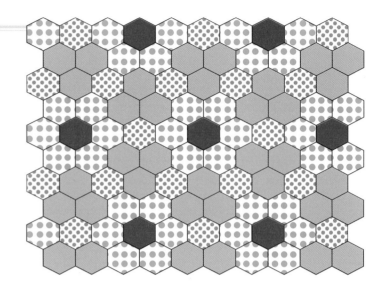

Percentages are special fractions – fractions where we split something into
100 pieces. This part of the patchwork quilt has 100 pieces and we can say
that 7% of them are red, 18% are purple and so on.

2

If we looked at a larger section of Mrs Martin's quilt, with
the same pattern but 200 pieces instead of 100, how many
pieces do you think would be red?

The same percentage would be red (7%), but because
we are looking at a larger section with 200 pieces,
there would be more actual pieces that are red!

7% means 7 **out of every 100**, so if there are 200
pieces altogether there would be twice as many
red pieces. We write this as:

$$7\% \text{ of } 200 = 14 \qquad \text{or} \qquad \frac{7}{100} \times 200 = 14$$

How many would be pink?

36% of 200 = ...

How many would be blue?

39% of 200 = ...

How many would be purple?

18% of 200 = ...

3

Using the divide button on a calculator, you
can change a percentage into a decimal.

$$18\% = \frac{18}{100} = 18 \div 100 = 0.18$$

Get a calculator and try these.

39% 39 ÷ 100 = ...

36% 36 ÷ 100 = ...

7%   7 ÷ 100 = ...

4

By changing percentages into decimals you can now work out more
difficult questions. If Mrs Martin's quilt had 250 pieces, you could work out
how many pieces were purple by finding 18% of 250. Find 18% by doing
this on your calculator:

18% of 250 = 18 divided by 100 and multiplied by 250 = 45 pieces

Try these: 36% of 250 = ... 25% of 640 = ... 75% of 480 = ...

5

People use percentages to compare scores and
results of tests or exams. These three children
go to different schools.

Tim was given a test with 15 questions. He got 9 correct.
Fiona was given a test with 100 questions and got 60 correct.
Pete was given a test with 90 questions and got 54 correct.

Who do you think did the best?

To find out, we work out the percentage mark for each one.

Tim got $\frac{9}{15}$ so we work out 9 ÷ 15 and multiply the number by
100 to get the percentage.

$\frac{9}{15} \times 100 = 60\%$ (Don't forget $\frac{9}{15}$ is the same as 9 ÷ 15!)

Find Fiona and Pete's percentages.

Fiona: $\frac{60}{100} \times 100 = $ ....%   Pete: $\frac{54}{90} \times 100 = $ ....%

Who scored the highest percentage? ....

What about Kevin who scored $\frac{3}{5}$? ....

Now turn over ➤

Now try these ...

1 Can you find the answers to these?

a What is 50% of 36? ....

b What is 10% of 60? ....

c What is 20% of 50? ....

d What is 75% of 200? ....

e What is 25% of 16? ....

f What is 100% of 200? ....

g What is 10% of 200? ....

h What is 25% of 120? ....

2 Can you work out these percentages?

a If there were 200 cars in a car park and 100 were red, what percentage were red cars? ....

b If there were 150 cars in a car park and 30 were blue, what percentage were blue cars? ....

c If there were 80 cars in a car park and 20 were white, what percentage were white cars? ....

3 Now try working out these.

a If there were 500 animals in a zoo and 200 of them were lions, what percentage were lions? ....

b If there were 500 animals in a zoo and 100 were monkeys, what percentage were monkeys? ....

c If there were 500 animals in a zoo and 10 were elephants, what percentage were elephants? ....

4 Which of these children did the best in their history tests? What were their percentage marks?

Ian scored $\frac{12}{15}$

Eleanor scored $\frac{35}{50}$

Joshua scored $\frac{9}{10}$

Percentage ....

Percentage ....

Percentage ....

Ahmed scored $\frac{79}{100}$

Rachel scored $\frac{54}{60}$

Chandu scored $\frac{4}{5}$

Percentage ....

Percentage ....

Percentage ....

More ways to help your child:

Point out examples of percentages in everyday life, for example newspapers, adverts, magazine surveys, sales.

Examine clothing labels for examples of percentage notation.

Transformers

Introduction:

Shape and space work is a prominent part of mathematics in the primary years. It is intended both as preparation for more formal geometry in secondary school and to help children develop 'spatial awareness' of the world around them.

An important tool for appreciating the properties of shapes is the idea of symmetry. **Reflective symmetry** (or line symmetry) is about the 'balance' of a shape, where the two halves are a mirror image of each other. Many mathematical shapes display this type of symmetry and it is therefore important for children to be able to recognise where it occurs. Similarly, many mathematical shapes possess **rotational symmetry**, where a shape is rotated through one or more right angles. Rotational symmetry can be shown practically with the aid of tracing paper and pins (see 'Teaching points' below). Reflection and rotation are types of **transformations**. A third type is **translation**, where a shape slides in any direction but without turning. Each occurrence of the letter 'b' on this page, for example, can be said to have been translated from the first 'b' that appeared on the page.

National Curriculum:

Attainment Target 3: Shape, Space and Measures

Key Stage 2 emphasises the importance of transformations. Children should:

*transform 2-D shapes by translation, reflection and rotation
and visualise movements and simple transformations to create patterns.*

Level 4 expects children to identify orders of rotational symmetry and to appreciate reflective symmetry. Level 5 extends the requirements to include translation.

Activity:

The activities in this Unit are concerned with transformations. Reflective symmetry was introduced in Book 2 and is briefly revisited as revision work. Two further types of transformation are then introduced – rotation and translation. Children's understanding of these ideas is then tested before a computer game is simulated which challenges them to find a route through a grid using reflection, rotation and translation. This work will enable them to appreciate the different ways in which two-dimensional (2-D) shapes can be moved, and will also help them to learn the name of each type of movement.

Teaching points:

Help your child to continue to visualise a shape as it is 'transformed' by moving cut out copies of the shape from the original position to the new or 'image' position. To show rotational symmetry, trace the outline of the shape, pin the tracing paper (usually at a corner) and rotate the paper.

Transformers

There are different ways we can
move and change flat shapes.

1

We can **reflect** the
shape in a mirror line.

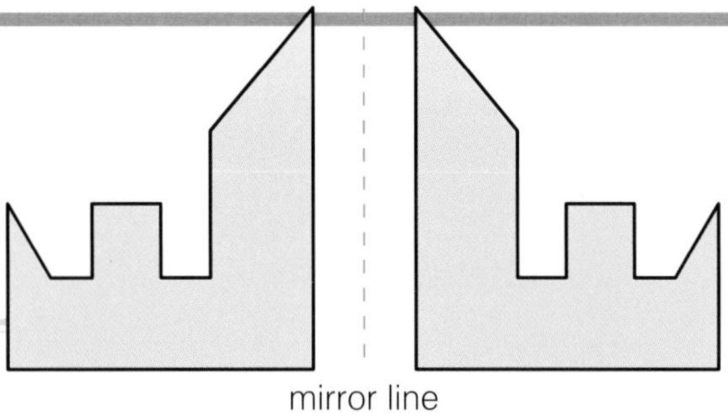

mirror line

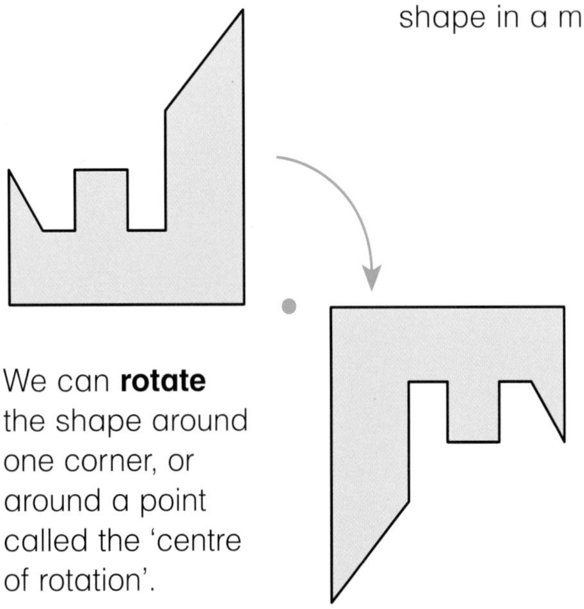

We can **rotate**
the shape around
one corner, or
around a point
called the 'centre
of rotation'.

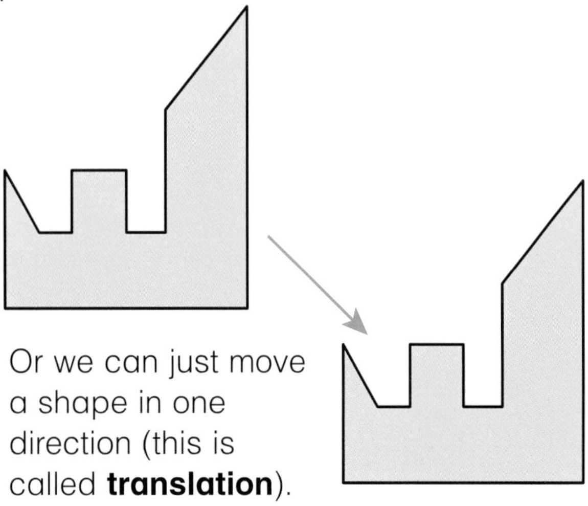

Or we can just move
a shape in one
direction (this is
called **translation**).

2

In the middle of this grid
is a dark green shape.
It has been changed or
moved to make the lighter
green shapes. Can you
work out how the darker
shape has been
transformed to make them?
Is it a **reflection**, **rotation**
or **translation**?

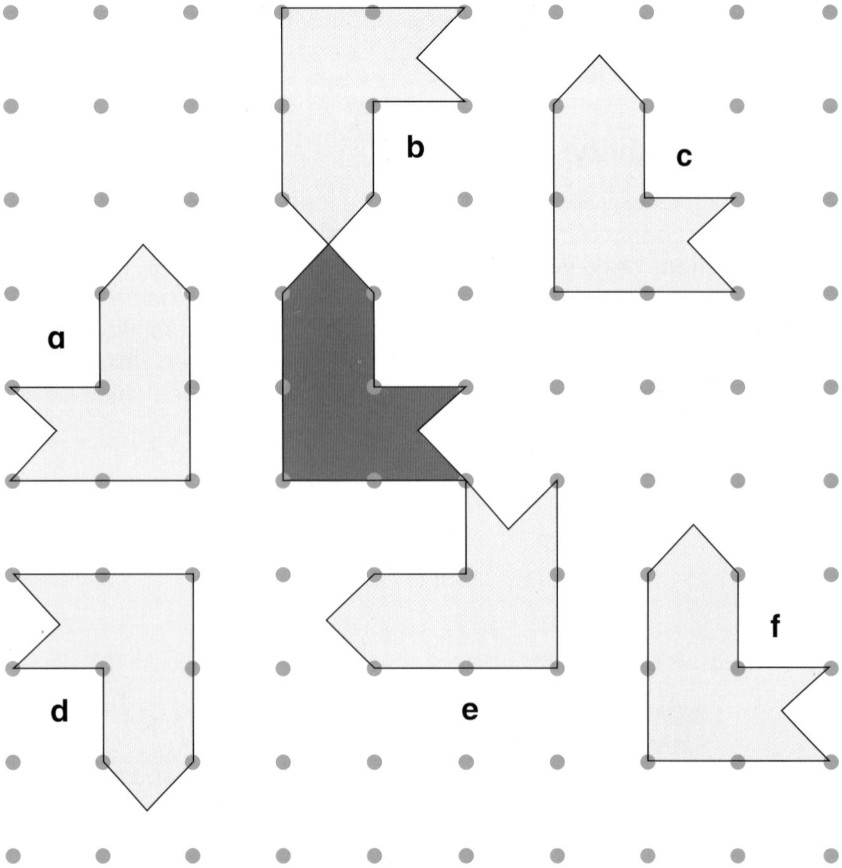

a ....

b ....

c ....

d ....

e ....

f ....

a

b

c

d

e

f

3

Neil is playing a computer game. The computer gives him instructions on how to move a duck through the maze below. (You will need to carefully trace and cut out the duck shape on page 55.)

1. Translation	1.
2. Reflection	2.
3. Rotation	3.
4. Reflection	4.
5. Translation	5.
6. Rotation	6.
7. Reflection	7.
8. Translation	8.
9. Rotation	9.
10. Rotation	10.

How to play

A translation in this game is a sideways, up or down, or diagonal movement to a next-door duck shape.

A rotation is a quarter turn about a corner on the duck itself.

A reflection is a mirror line on one side of the duck.

Work out the route the duck must take from the start to the finish.

Write on the computer screen the instructions for a different route back.

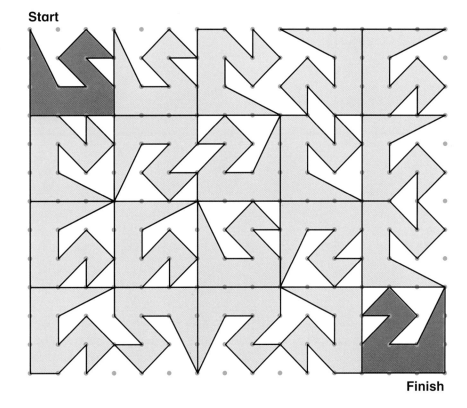

Start

Finish

Now turn over ➤

Now try these ...

Can you identify the type of transformation each shape has done?

1 ....

2 ....

3 ....

4 ....

5 ....

Balancing act

Introduction:

Algebra is a branch of maths which uses symbols, often letters of the alphabet, to **stand for numbers**. This is an important point to appreciate. We often use letters in arithmetic (10p, 3m and 200g), but they are simply abbreviations for pence or metre etc. The use of letters in algebra has a different purpose. They represent a number. Early work often uses the idea of a letter standing for a specific, or **constant**, number as in $x + 3 = 5$. Here we can see that x is 2. Later work extends this to the more sophisticated idea of a **variable**. When we write $3x + 2y = 20$ we mean that the x is an unknown amount, of which we have three and which, combined with two lots of a different unknown, makes 20. We use the term 'variable' because there are many possible values for x and y in this equation, for example x could be 6 and y could be 1, or x could be 2 and y could be 7 (an equation is simply a statement that uses an equals sign).

National Curriculum:

Attainment Target 2: Number and Algebra

At Key Stage 2 the National Curriculum states that children should be using algebraic ideas:

expressed initially in words and then using letters as symbols.

Level 4 expects children to use simple formulas expressed in words. Level 5 requires children to do this using letters as variables.

Activity:

The activities in this Unit introduce the idea of using letters to stand for numbers. This is done initially using a 'constant' as in $x + 5 = 8$ where there is a single number for x. This is then developed through a practical shape activity to explore the idea that a letter can stand for a range of numbers, as in $x + y = 10$. Children make three-dimensional (3-D) shapes (using cocktail sticks and jelly sweets or straws and Plasticine etc.) before counting the number of faces, vertices (corners) and edges each has. The idea of a balance is used to develop an equation into which children can insert new numbers and apply these to different shapes. The equation is rewritten in a variety of ways, using the idea of balance scales, within the real context of making shapes to make the work meaningful.

Teaching points:

Explore the idea of 'constants' with your child in oral questions such as, 'If 6 plus y is 11, what is y?' and 'I'm thinking of a mystery number called x, which, when I take 3 from it, leaves 15. What is my number?'

The idea that a variety of numbers can be substituted for a letter can be explored with puzzles such as 'Think of any number between 1 and 10, add 2, multiply by 5, subtract 10 and divide by 5 and add 1. Tell me the number you are left with and I'll tell you the number you started with.' Here the final number will always be one more than the start number.

Balancing act

Emily has a pop-up maths book with things to lift, pull and turn. To find the answers she must pull the tab, lift the flap and turn the wheel!

Pull the tab.

$3 +$ a $= 5$

1

Each of the questions in her book has a letter in it: **a**, **b**, and **c**. You have to guess what number the letter is standing for to make the sum 'balance'.

What is on one side of the equals sign is worth the same as what is on the other side. So **3 + a** is worth the same as **5**. To make it balance **a** must be **2**!

What numbers do **b** and **c** stand for?

b = ...   c = ...

Lift the flap.

b $+ 2 = 8 + 2$

Turn the wheel.

$1 +$ c $= 4 + 5$

Thinking of the question as being like a set of balance scales can be helpful.

2

Sometimes a letter can stand for more than one number. If we had a question such as **x + y = 10**, whatever **x** stood for would depend on what **y** stood for.

Look at this: **x + y = 10**

If x was 0 $0 + y = 10$ ...   so y would have to be 10.
If x was 1 $1 + y = 10$ ...   so y would have to be 9.
If x was 2 $2 + y = 10$ ...   so y would have to be 8.
If x was 3 $3 + y = 10$ ...   so y would have to be 7.
If x was 4 $4 + y = 10$ ...   so y would have to be 6.

Continue the pattern on a separate piece of paper.

If x was 5 ...

3

Use cocktail sticks and Plasticine or jelly sweets to make these 3-D shapes.

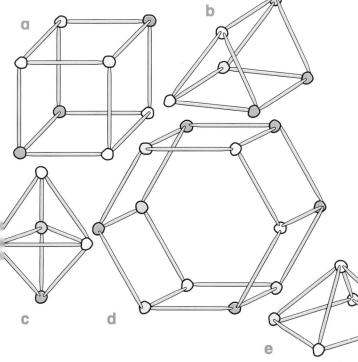

Shape	Number of faces	Number of vertices	Number of edges
a			
b			
c			
d			
e			

Fill in the table for each shape you make.

To count the **faces** imagine how many flat pieces of cardboard you would need to cover the shape.

To count the **vertices**, count the lumps of Plasticine, or jelly sweets.

The **edges** are the cocktail sticks.

Look at the table and see if you can see any patterns in the numbers.

4

Here is a set of balance scales. On one side is the number of faces and vertices, and on the other is the number of edges plus 2.

F + V   E + 2

Use the numbers from the table above and see if the scales will balance for each shape, like this:

$$6 + 8 = 12 + 2$$
$$14 = 14$$

Does it work for the other shapes?

....

....

....

This '**formula**', F + V = E + 2, can be rearranged by adding or taking away a number or letter from each side. If we do the same to both sides, the scales will balance.

Here we are taking away 2 from each side:

$$F + V - 2 = E + 2 - 2$$

In this case + 2 – 2 = 0 so we get …

$$F + V - 2 = E$$

Will the scales balance with **this** formula using numbers from the table above?

....

Now turn over ➤

Now try these ...

1 What does the letter stand for in these questions?

a 3 + x = 7   x = ...   e 5 + y = 12   y = ...   i 8 + a = 15   a = ...

b 14 – b = 3   b = ...   f 23 – x = 16   x = ...   j 14 – y = 0   y = ...

c x + 6 = 18   x = ...   g y + 9 = 24   y = ...   k b + 6 = 24   b = ...

d c – 10 = 5   c = ...   h p – 14 = 24   p = ...   l x – 20 = 0   x = ...

2 Can you find all the answers to this equation?

x + y = 12

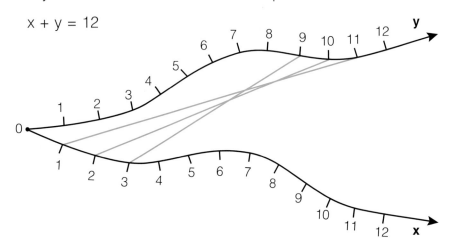

Join up the 'values' for x and y on the curvy axes. Three have been done for you.

3 Take away E from both sides, to rearrange the formula.

F + V = E + 2 ....

Take away V from both sides, to rearrange the formula.

F + V = E + 2 ....

Take away F from both sides, to rearrange the formula.

F + V = E + 2 ....

(Check the new formulas balance by using the numbers from the table on the previous page.)

More ways to help your child:

Talk to your child about 'formulas' you use in everyday life, for example how do you convert litres into gallons, kilograms into pounds? Conversion tables can be found in cookery books, garages and supermarkets.

Measuring units

Introduction:

Children need to be able to choose the correct units to measure length, area, perimeter, volume, capacity, weight, temperature, angle and time. They also need to see the inter-relationship between units, for example 1 litre of water weighs 1 kilogram. Children also need to be able to read measuring scales correctly. These may be marked in whole number intervals, such as 2, 5, 10, 50 and 100; calibrated using fractions, such as $\frac{1}{2}$, $\frac{1}{4}$, $\frac{3}{4}$; or in decimals with 0.1, 0.2 or 0.5.

National Curriculum:

Attainment Target 2: Shape, Space and Measures

The National Curriculum at Key Stage 2 states that children should:

choose and use appropriate measuring instruments; interpret numbers and read scales to an increasing degree of accuracy.

Children should also: *choose appropriate units and make sensible estimations with them in everyday situations, and extend their understanding of the relationships between units.*

Level 4 asks children to choose and use appropriate measuring units and to read the scales of a variety of measuring instruments. Level 5 expects children to be able to convert one metric unit into another and to have some familiarity with imperial units still in everyday use.

Activity:

The initial activities require children to match measuring instruments with measuring topics, as in selecting cubes to measure volume, and also to match units of measurement with topics. It is important that children are able to know that length, for example, can be measured in millimetres, centimetres and metres etc. but not in grams, litres or degrees. The third activity is concerned with improving children's ability to read and interpret measuring scales. The term 'scales' here is not to be confused with (or limited to) a set of kitchen scales used to weigh flour etc. Rulers, thermometers, measuring jugs and protractors are all 'scales'. The activity focuses on the intervals into which a scale is divided. These could be in ones, tens, hundreds or tenths etc. and it is vital that children understand how a particular scale is calibrated if they are to use it successfully.

Teaching points:

Emphasise the importance of looking carefully at the intervals into which the scales are divided. Your child may well need help to do this successfully.

Discuss the importance of choosing the correct units when measuring.

Measuring units

Mr Measurer is sorting out his cupboards.

1

He has decided to sort his equipment and measuring instruments into labelled boxes. Can you help him decide which items go where? Draw a line, or arrow, to join the instruments to the right box. One has been done for you.

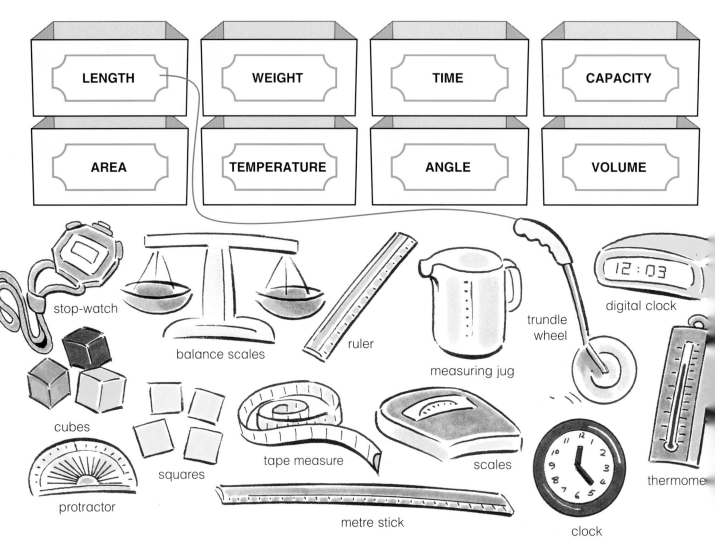

LENGTH WEIGHT TIME CAPACITY

AREA TEMPERATURE ANGLE VOLUME

stop-watch balance scales ruler measuring jug trundle wheel digital clock

cubes squares tape measure scales protractor metre stick clock thermome

2

We can use many different units to describe measurements. If we are measuring **length**, we might use metres or centimetres. If we are measuring **time**, we might use seconds or minutes.

Can you sort out which of these units are used to measure: length, weight, time, capacity, area, temperature, angle and volume? Write a list for each one on a separate piece of paper.

kilograms (kg)	minutes (min)
degrees (°)	cubic centimetres (cm^3)
metres (m)	litres (l)
kilometres (km)	square metres (m^2)
hours (hr)	degrees Celsius (°C)
seconds (s)	centimetres (cm)
grams (g)	millilitres (ml)

3

Sometimes the hardest part of measuring is reading the scale. Some scales have a mark for every single number. But on other scales putting a mark for every number would be too crowded.

Look carefully at the measurements shown on these scales.

To work out the measurement, find the 'difference' between two next door numbers. (On scale **a** the difference between 10 and 0 is 10!)

Then see how many spaces (or intervals) there are between those two marks. (On scale **a** there are 5 intervals.)

To find out how much each interval is worth, divide the difference in the marks by the number of intervals. (For example, 10 ÷ 5 = 2. So each interval on scale **a** is worth 2.)

Write down all the readings on these scales. Remember to say what units they are.

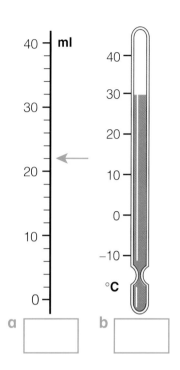

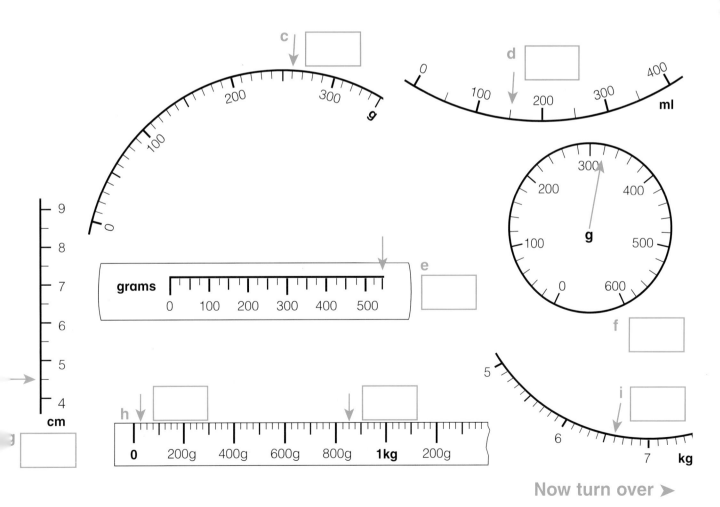

Now turn over ➤

Now try these ...

1   Can you match the units to their correct topics?

cm   **area**   mm   g   **length**

metre   **weight**   degree   **capacity** cm^3

cm^2 **volume**   litre   **angle** m^2

kg m^3 mile   km

2   Continue these patterns.

0	.....	10	.....	20	25	30	.....	.....	.....	50
100	120	.....	160	.....	200	.....	.....	260	.....	.....
50	.....	150	200	.....	.....	350	.....	.....	.....	550
0	0.5	.....	1.5	.....	.....	3.0	3.5	.....	.....	.....
0	.....	0.5	.....	1.0	.....	.....	.....	2.0	2.25	.....

3   What numbers do these scales show? Remember to say what unit they are.

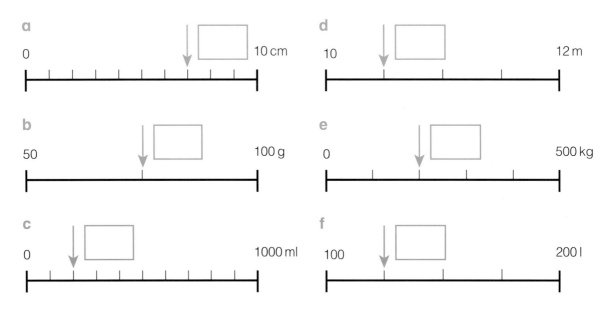

a   0   10 cm

b   50   100 g

c   0   1000 ml

d   10   12 m

e   0   500 kg

f   100   200 l

More ways to help your child:

Get your child to use any measuring instruments you have around the house – weighing scales in the kitchen or bathroom, tape measures, thermometers, stop-watches etc. – to gain a familiarity with their uses, units and intervals.

Try angles

Introduction:

Children need to realise that any drawn angle is part of a turn – that the two 'arms' of an angle start together, initially overlapping each other, before one opens out a certain amount. This idea can be demonstrated by opening a book and showing the angle that has been created. Children need to understand this in order to be able to use a protractor, because it is based on the notion of an angle as a turn. A typical symptom of a lack of understanding is the inability to decide which set of measurements on the protractor to use, with the result that an angle of 60° is misread as 120°.

National Curriculum:

Attainment Target 3: Shape, Space and Measures

The National Curriculum at Key Stage 2 states that children should be taught to:

*use right angles, fractions of a turn and, later, degrees
to measure rotation, and use the associated language.*

Level 5 expects children to be drawing and measuring angles to the nearest degree and to be familiar with the language associated with angles. This includes such terms as acute, right, obtuse, straight and reflex angles, all of which are explained below.

Activity:

The first activity in this Unit reminds children that angles are turns by getting them to make and use a simple angle measurer (using card and a paper fastener as described on page 55). Further activities focus on measuring angles within triangles. The idea of degrees as a unit of measurement is introduced and then linked to the different types of angle: **acute** – less than 90°, **right** – exactly 90°, **obtuse** – more than 90° but less than 180°, **straight** – exactly 180° and **reflex** – more than 180°. Triangles are examined in terms of these and children are introduced to the idea of the interior angles of a triangle adding up to 180°. The protractor is discussed in terms of the turning work covered both here and in Book 3.

Teaching points:

Emphasise the relationship between the static drawing of angles on paper and turning as discussed in the 'Introduction' above.

Should your child have difficulty in deciding which degree scale to choose on the protractor, you will need to re-emphasise how the angle is created – the arms of the angle begin by lying on top of each other at 0° (no angle) before one opens out.

Try angles

For this section you will need to copy and make the angle measurer as described on page 55.

1

Using your newly made angle measurer, see if you can work out which of the angles at the corners of these triangles are **acute**, **obtuse** or **right angles**. Some have been filled in to help you with the others.

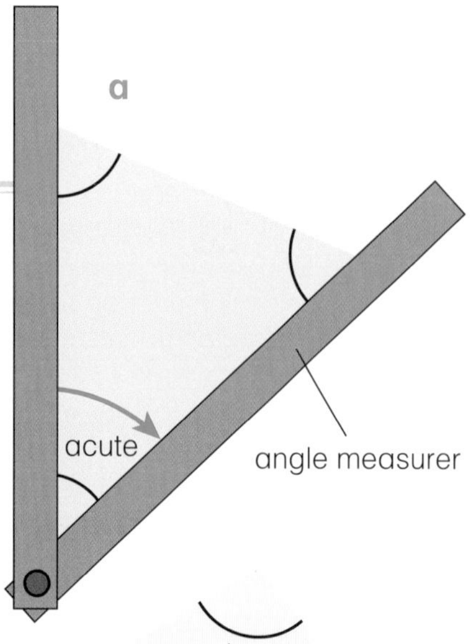

a

acute

angle measurer

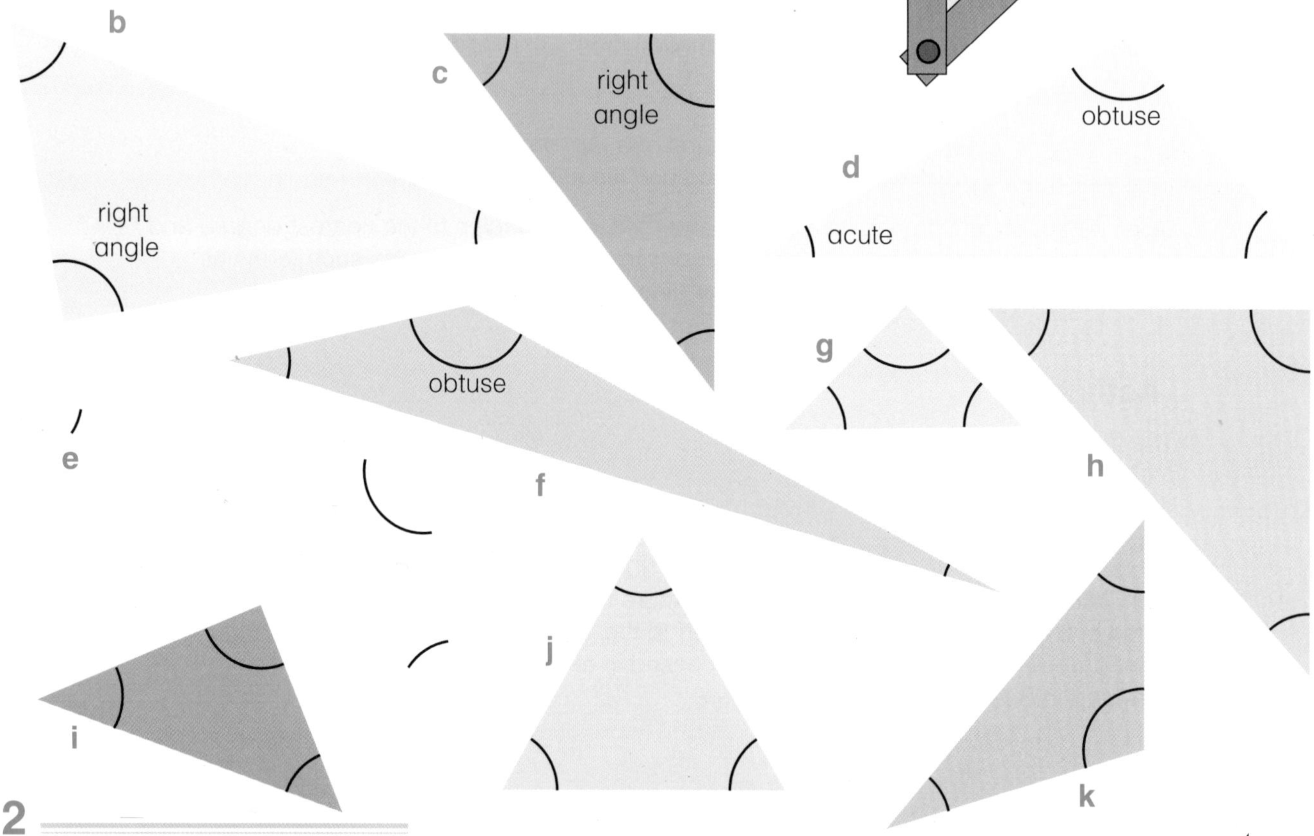

obtuse

b

c

right angle

d

right angle

acute

obtuse

g

e

f

h

i

j

k

2

There are special names for different sorts of triangles.

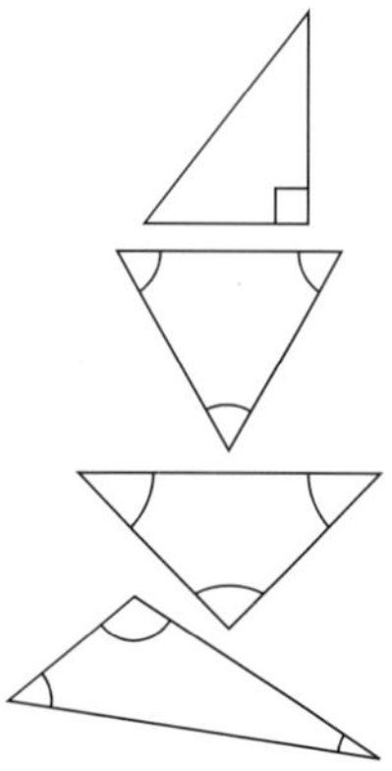

A **right-angled** triangle is one with a right angle at one of the corners.
An **equilateral** triangle is one with three identical angles and three sides the same length.
An **isosceles** triangle is one with two identical angles and two of the three sides the same length.
A **scalene** triangle is one with three different angles and three sides with different lengths.

To be sure which of the triangles are which, you need to learn how to measure angles exactly using a protractor.

3

To measure an angle, place the centre mark of a protractor on the corner of the angle. Line up the protractor line marked 0 with one of the angle lines. Count round from 0 to where the other angle line is. In this case, the angle is 50 **degrees**, which we write as 50°.

The angle at one corner of the purple triangle below is an obtuse angle. When measuring obtuse angles be careful to count around from 0, all the way past 90 to where the other angle line is. In this case, the angle is 120 degrees (**not** 60).

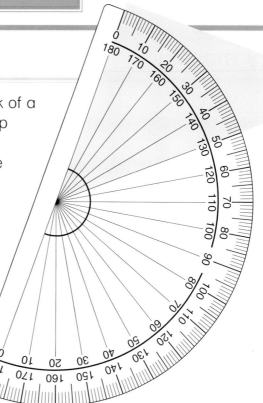

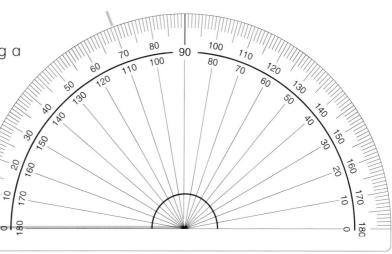

4

Measure all the angles at the corners of the triangles in Question 1.

Try adding together the three angles of each triangle. What do you notice about the numbers? The angles inside a triangle, if you've measured correctly, should always add up to 180 degrees. Check yours to see if they are correct!

5

To draw an angle, start with drawing a line and placing your protractor on top, with the centre mark at one end of the line. Count round to the angle required and put a small mark. Remove the protractor and draw a line joining the new mark to the end of the line. This is how you would draw an angle of 70°.

Now turn over ➤

Now try these ...

1   Measure these angles. Describe what type of angle each is (acute, obtuse etc.).

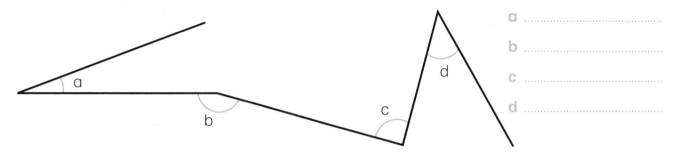

a ....

b ....

c ....

d ....

2   Work out the size of the third angle in these triangles and describe what type of triangle
each is (right-angled, equilateral, isosceles, scalene).

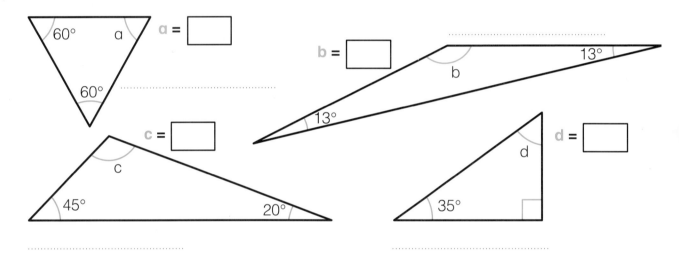

a = ☐

....

c = ☐

b = ☐

....

d = ☐

....

3   Draw these angles.

10°   **77°**   **100°**   **165°**

From time to time

Introduction:

The old adage 'time flies when you're having fun' is very real for children, for whom time seems to pass at varying speeds depending on how enjoyable the current experience is. The fact that time passes at a constant rate is learnt through experience. Children need to develop a 'feel' for the length of the units in which time is measured, so as to know roughly how long a minute or half an hour is. In this age of digital watches, children can often say the time, for example 'Ten forty-five' without any real sense of what this means. As fewer traditional clock-faces are seen around town or at home, so the need for children to develop this sense of time becomes more important. Book 2 contained a variety of activities designed to promote these ideas. By the end of their junior years children should be beginning to show sufficient familiarity with the units in which time is measured (seconds, minutes etc.) to be able to convert from one to another and be able to add and subtract times, as in 3 hours 22 minutes plus 4 hours 56 minutes.

National Curriculum:

Attainment Target 3: Shape, Space and Measures

The National Curriculum at Key Stage 2 requires children to:

choose appropriate units of time and make sensible estimates
with them in everyday situations, and to
extend their understanding of the relationship between units.

Level 4 refers to the ability to tell the time. Level 5 expects children to convert between units of time, for example hours, minutes and seconds.

Activity:

The early part of this Unit is concerned with the units in which time is measured and children's ability to convert between these – both the conversion of hours and minutes to minutes, and also minutes and seconds to seconds. The activities are placed in the contexts of stop-watches and video machines to help give meaning to the material. The final activity considers the addition and subtraction of time, again placed in context, in this case using the length of music tracks on a CD.

Teaching points:

Your child may have difficulty in adding and subtracting times, such as 3 hr 22 min plus 4 hr 56 min because the minutes are based on sixties. As a result your child may arrive at the answer 7 hr 78 min without having realised the need to swap 60 of those minutes for one hour.

From time to time

Do you ever time yourself? How long does it take you to get to school? How fast can you run upstairs? How long does it take your hair to grow one centimetre?

1

We can measure time using units such as seconds, minutes, hours, days, weeks and years.

Here a stop-watch is being used to time some races in a swimming pool. The races are timed in **seconds**.

Look at the winning times for the 100 m races. How long are 65 s and 122 s? Are they over or under a minute?

Use this table to help you:

1 min	2 min	3 min	4 min	5 min
60 s	120 s	180 s	240 s	300 s

WINNERS		
50 m	front crawl	31 s
100 m	front crawl	65 s
50 m	breast-stroke	58 s
100 m	breast-stroke	122 s

We can give times as just seconds, or as minutes and seconds, like this:

65 s = 1 min, 5 s   **122 s = 2 min, 2 s**

Write these times in the same way.

75 s ....   90 s ....   130 s ....

181 s ....   119 s ....   250 s ....

260 s ....   222 s ....   360 s ....

2

Here is a video recorder and some video tapes. On the boxes of the tapes are the lengths of recording time, shown in **minutes**. The numbers in brackets indicate the times of the tapes if your video recorder can record on 'long play' (where it can record twice as much on one tape).

Use this table to help you work out the times in hours.

1 hr	2 hr	3 hr	4 hr	5 hr	6 hr
60 min	120 min	180 min	240 min	300 min	360 min

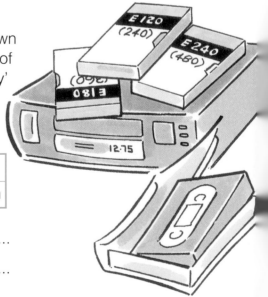

120 min.............   180 min.............   240 min...............

(240) ....   (360) ....   (480) ....

3

Change these times to minutes.

3 hr 58 min = ...   5 hr 11 min = ...

2 hr 42 min = ...   1 hr 41 min = ...

6 hr 5 min = ...

4

Here is a CD. On the back it gives the times of each track, or song, on the CD.

1) Have I told you lately?	4:30	(4 minutes, 30 seconds)
2) Boogie Woogie Stomp	3:10	
3) Maggie May	5:05	
4) All I want is blackbean soup	2:50	
5) Gallan's Boogie	6:48	
6) Hey Jude	4:13	

If you want to find how long two tracks would take to play, you need to add the times together. But you have to be careful. Can you see why?

Track 2 + Track 4 = 3:10 (3 minutes, 10 seconds)

+ 2:50 (2 minutes, 50 seconds)

When you add 10 seconds and 50 seconds you get 60 seconds, which is a minute!

So the answer to Track 2 + Track 4 is 3 + 2 + 1 = 6 minutes.

Try adding these:

Track 1 + Track 2 = ...

Track 4 + Track 6 = ...

Track 3 + Track 5 = ...

Track 5 + Track 6 = ...

All the tracks together = ...

If you had only 10 minutes, which tracks could you listen to?

....

....

....

There are 5 seconds silence before each track. If you chose to listen to all the tracks in order, which track would be playing exactly 16 minutes after the start?

....

Now turn over ➤

Now try these ...

1   Change these times from minutes to **hours and minutes**.

120 minutes   ....   115 minutes   ....

75 minutes   ....   135 minutes   ....

180 minutes   ....   222 minutes   ....

270 minutes   ....   380 minutes   ....

2   Change these times from hours and minutes to **minutes**.

1 hr 10 min   ....   1 hr 15 min   ....

1 hr 40 min   ....   2 hr 35 min   ....

3 hr 5 min   ....   2 hr 45 min   ....

3 hr 40 min   ....   3 hr 0 min   ....

3   Mr Large is travelling from East Grinstead to London.

Can you fill in the rest of this timetable?

All the trains follow the same route and take the same time to make the journey.

Leaves East Grinstead	Arrives Oxted	Arrives East Croydon	Arrives London
5.30 am	5.45 am	6.15 am	7.00 am
8.30 am			
8.45 am			
10.00 am			
1.05 pm			
4.42 pm			
6.55 pm			
8.15 pm			
10.33 pm			

More ways to help your child:

Use TV listings to get your child to work out the lengths of films etc. in hours and minutes and in minutes alone.

Use CD and record covers to provide other opportunities for work on time. For example, 'What is the total playing time?', 'How much longer is the longest track than the shortest?'

Key questions

Introduction:

We can accurately locate any point by using just two numbers, and these numbers are the **co-ordinates** of that point. Two number lines, or axes, are drawn at right angles to each other. The horizontal line is known as the x axis and the vertical is the y axis (children often remember this through the phrase, 'y is high', and they should be familiar with the idea of axes from previous work on graphs). The point at which the axes meet, labelled (0,0), is called the **origin**. By moving first along the x axis and then along the y axis we are able to specify a unique point on the grid. The co-ordinates for such a point are written, for example, as (3, 2) and mean three units along the x axis followed by two along the y. This order of x before y is vital and it can be remembered alphabetically in terms of 'across before up', that is 'a' before 'u' or even 'in the house, up the stairs'.

The co-ordinate system identifies points on a surface rather than areas, such as squares. Children's early work often uses a system that labels a square rather than a point (as on street plans). This system may also use letters along one axis, so (B, 3) would show a square on the map in which a street was located. While not being a true co-ordinate system, work which uses this method of labelling is valuable both as a means of understanding such street plans, and also as a forerunner to more formal co-ordinate work.

National Curriculum:

Attainment Target 3: Shape, Space and Measures

The National Curriculum at Key Stage 2 requires children to:

use co-ordinates to specify location, for example
map references and the representation of 2-D shapes.

Level 4 expects children to draw 2-D shapes in different orientations on grids.

Activity:

The activities in this Unit introduce the idea of identifying a position using co-ordinates. The ideas behind the co-ordinate system are explained and necessary vocabulary is introduced, including x and y co-ordinates and axes. There is the opportunity to develop the skills needed to plot points on a grid, in particular the need to realise that the x co-ordinate is always given first. Further practice activities include a 'grape-squashing' game and a question in which children are asked to plot a set of given co-ordinates and then reverse them, so that (6,3) becomes (3,6), and then to plot this new set. The resulting points provide a link with an earlier Unit on transformations (pages 23–26) in that they are an example of reflective symmetry.

Teaching points:

Emphasise the importance of the **order** of the numbers in co-ordinates and the need to move along the x axis first. A further way of remembering this is the pun, 'x is a cross'.

Key questions

The Key Questions quiz show has prizes hidden behind locked doors. Contestants answer questions and give the co-ordinates of a keyhole to win a prize. But they can't see what is behind those doors!

1

To identify a keyhole the contestants use **co-ordinates**, which are two numbers inside a set of brackets, like this (3,1). The **first** number in the brackets is known as the **x co-ordinate** and tells how many places **across** to move.

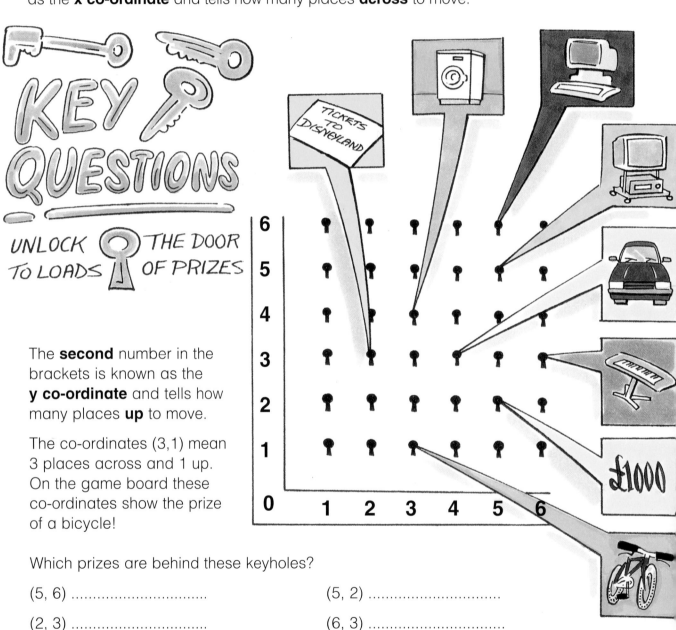

The **second** number in the brackets is known as the **y co-ordinate** and tells how many places **up** to move.

The co-ordinates (3,1) mean 3 places across and 1 up. On the game board these co-ordinates show the prize of a bicycle!

Which prizes are behind these keyholes?

(5, 6) ....

(2, 3) ....

(4, 3) ....

(5, 2) ....

(6, 3) ....

(5, 5) ....

Can you write the co-ordinates for the washing machine? ....
Check your answer is different from the co-ordinates for the car!

2

The Great Grape Game

A game for two or more players.

Each player draws a grid (like the game board opposite), using squared paper. Draw and number the two lines (the **x axis** is across and the **y axis** is up). Each player draws six grapes secretly on their own grid and writes the co-ordinates next to them.

Take it in turns to try to squash each other's grapes by rolling the dice twice – the first number is the x co-ordinate, and the second is the y co-ordinate.

The winner is the last player with any grapes left unsquashed!

3

Plot these co-ordinates and join the crosses as you go along. You might find something a little 'ruff'!

(8, 9)   (6, 9)   (5, 8)   (5, 6)   (4, 6)

(4, 8)   (2, 8)   (2, 6)   (1, 6)   (1, 9)

(0, 8)   (0, 9)   (1, 10)   (5, 10)   (7, 12)

(7, 11)   (8, 10)   (8, 9)

Now reverse the x and y co-ordinates and fill in the new co-ordinates here.

(9, 8)   (9, 6)   (,)   (,)   (,)

(,)   (,)   (,)   (,)   (,)

(,)   (,)   (,)   (,)   (,)

(,)   (,)   (,)

Plot these points on the grid opposite. What do you notice?

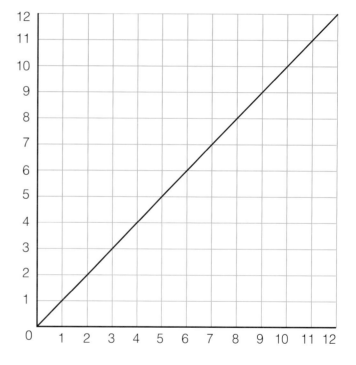

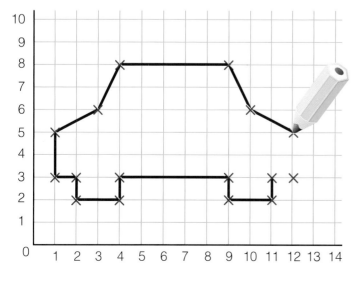

4

Draw a simple picture on squared paper and carefully write down the co-ordinates in order. You might like to try a picture of a car.

Give the co-ordinates to your friends to see if they can guess what it is!

Now turn over ➤

45

Now try these ...

1 Mark these co-ordinates on the grid below. What picture do they create?

(11,1)   (11,4)   (13,4)   (13,1)
(15,1)   (15,9)   (13,11) (13,12)
(12,12) (12,11) (4,11)   (2,9)
(2,1)   (11,1)

Draw on some windows. Write the co-ordinates for them here.

....

....

....

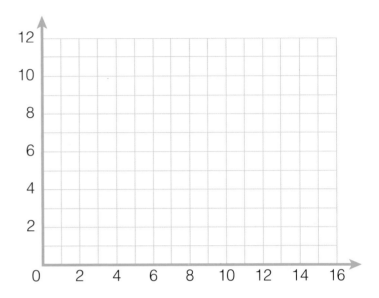

2 Now try these co-ordinates.

(5,1)   (10,1) (13,3) (14,5) (14,6)
(13,8) (11,10) (10,10) (8,9)   (8,10)
(9,11) (9,12) (8,11) (7,9)   (5,10)
(4,10) (2,8)   (1,6)   (1,5)   (2,3)
(5,1)

Draw a leaf next to the stalk. Write the co-ordinates for the leaf here.

....

....

Use some squared paper to draw your own co-ordinate pictures.

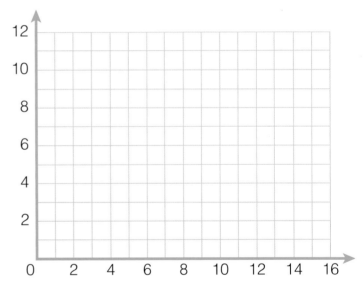

More ways to help your child:

Many types of map, particularly Ordnance Survey maps, offer plenty of opportunities for co-ordinate practice. Your child can locate places he or she knows by using a map of the local area.

Ask your child to choose a simple shape, such as a square or a right-angled triangle, and draw it several times on a grid. Then write down the co-ordinates of the vertices (corners). Your child can then look for patterns in the numbers written down.

What does 'mean' mean?

Introduction:

Children were given the opportunity to represent data using pictograms, block graphs and line graphs and asked to interpret these in earlier books. This Unit revisits these graphs and includes another graph, the pie chart. Circular pie charts are often used when we want to show the proportions of things rather than their actual amounts.

The main focus of this Unit is an examination of the different types of averages. The **mode** is the item or number that appears most often in a set of data. The **median** is the middle value of a set of numbers that have been arranged in order of size, for example the median of 2, 3, 5, 8, 9 is 5. If there is an even number of values the median is half-way between the two middle ones, for example the median of 2, 4, 6, 7 is 5. Should the two middle values be the same, that value is the median. The **mean** is what is usually referred to as 'the average', that is a list of numbers added together and divided by how many numbers there are in the list. The **range** is the difference between the highest and lowest value in a set of data.

The use of the mean can be both informative and deceptive. Consider the fact that the mean number of legs people have in this country is fewer than two! This is because although no one has three, some people (enough to drop the mean below two) have only one or none at all. This example shows why different types of averages are required – one can be more appropriate to a situation than another.

National Curriculum:

Attainment Target 4: Handling Data

The National Curriculum at Key Stage 2 expects children to:

> *collect and represent data appropriately using graphs and diagrams, including block graphs and line graphs, and interpret a wider range of graphs including pie charts.*

Level 4 expects children to collect, represent and interpret discrete data, to include the use of line graphs and to use the ideas of mode and median. Level 5 extends this to include pie charts and the use of the mean.

Activity:

The initial activities in this Unit help children to understand what the resulting mean number represents. Mode and median are then revisited and, together with the mean, are explored through contexts familiar to children. The fourth activity highlights the different types of graph we can use to represent data. A pictogram and a block graph are illustrated, each using 'discrete' data, i.e. things that can be counted, such as cars, birds or coins. A line graph follows, showing 'continuous' data, i.e. things that can be measured, such as temperature or weight (see Book 2 for more information on these ideas). Finally, a pie chart is shown indicating proportion, in this case what proportion, out of the whole number of birds seen, were robins, or blue tits, or sparrows etc.

Teaching points:

Encourage your child to explore data found in everyday life – newspapers, TV adverts, comics etc. and ask your child to explain the meaning of any simple graphs found.

Use the term axis (plural axes) when discussing graphs. The axes are the vertical and horizontal lines on which the scale is marked.

What does 'mean' mean?

Do you know what the word 'mean' means in maths?

1

Here is a table showing how many sweets Lucy was given in a week. On Monday she was given 5 sweets, on Tuesday she was given 6 … and so on. How many sweets was she given over the whole week? ....

Lucy decided not to eat her sweets that week. Instead of having more sweets some days than others, she decided to spead them out over the next week so she had the same number each day. She worked this out by counting them (21) and then sharing them out equally between 7 days. In other words, 21 ÷ 7 = 3. So she had 3 sweets each day.

In maths, we call this the **mean** number of sweets.

M	Tu	W	Th	F	Sat	Sun
5	6	0	2	1	4	3
3	3	3	3	3	3	3

2

This is how much money Lucy was given over six weeks.

Week 1	£2	Week 4	£5
Week 2	£4	Week 5	£2
Week 3	£2	Week 6	£3

She decides to spread the money out equally so she has the same for each week. This is the **mean** amount of money.

To work it out, find the total amount of money and divide by the number of weeks.

Mean value = £ ....

The **mean** value is a type of average.
Do you know the names of other types of average?

The **median** value is the number, when all the data is put in order, that is exactly in the middle.

The **mode** is the number that occurs most often, or the most chosen item.

3

Lucy works out that the **mean** value is £3, as it is £18 shared evenly over 6 weeks (18 ÷ 6 = 3). The **median** value is £2.50, because when we order the amount of money like this:

2   2   2   3   4   5

the middle two values are 2 and 3. So we take the number half-way between the two. The **mode** is £2 because it is the value that occurs most often.

Here is a list of spelling test scores from some children in a class.

8   18   13   10   10   9   17   14   12   10   11

What is the mean score? ....

What is the median score? (Remember to order the numbers first!) ....

What is the mode (or modal) score? ....

The **range** of scores can also be worked out, by subtracting the lowest score from the highest.
What is the range of these scores? ....

4

Here is some information represented in different ways. Can you write three sentences on another piece of paper about each graph or chart? For example, how many birds were seen? Were there more robins than blackbirds? What time of the day is warmest?

Pictogram

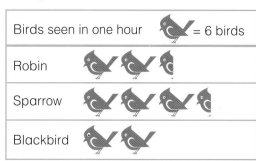

Block graph

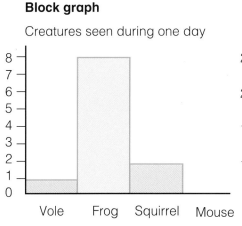

Line graph

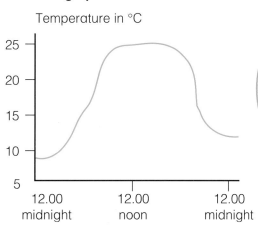

Pie chart

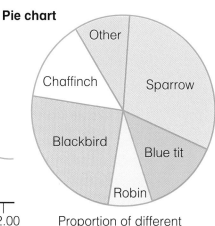

Proportion of different birds seen in one day

Now turn over ➤

Now try these ...

1   a Here is a list of test scores from some children in school.

3   4   4   5   5   5   7   8   8   9   12   15   19

What is the **range** of scores?............   What is the **mean** score? ....

What is the **median** score ? ....   What is the **mode** (or **modal**) score? ....

   b Next month, after lots of hard work, their scores were:

6   7   8   9   11   11   11   12   13   17   17   17   17

What is the **range** of scores? ....   What is the **mean** score? ....

What is the **median** score ? ....   What is the **mode** (or **modal**) score? ....

2   Find a recent list of football results, perhaps from a Sunday paper.

What are the **mean**, **median** and **mode** number of goals scored in the Premier League? (Use a calculator if you want.)

What is the **range** number of goals scored in the Premier League?

Compare these figures with another league, such as Division 3.

Are there any differences? Why do you think this might be?

3   Here is a list of the daily earnings of some workers in a supermarket. There are 10 cleaners, 40 stackers and 1 manager.

Cleaners £25   Stackers £34   Manager £73

The average pay per day is £33.

   a Which average has been used here? ....

   b Which average produces the answer £34? ....

   c What would the answer to the third type of average be? ....

Magic maths

Introduction:

Probability is concerned with chance in the sense of **estimating the likelihood** of events taking place. Children need to develop ideas about probability from both experience and experiment. Book 3 introduced children to probability based on experience, such as trying to forecast the weather, and that based on mathematical experiment, such as the chances of rolling a dice to get a 6.

This Unit develops previous work by analysing the outcomes of events and giving them a numerical value. The probability scale in Book 3 assessed the outcomes of events in terms of 'likely', 'unlikely', 'no chance' etc. but this Unit develops this into a more precise numerical scale. The probability of rolling a 1 on a dice is $\frac{1}{6}$, because there are six possible outcomes, one of which is to roll a 1. Similarly, the probability of rolling a 2 is $\frac{1}{6}$, while the chances of an even number are $\frac{3}{6}$ or $\frac{1}{2}$. Probability can be expressed as a number using either fractions or decimals.

National Curriculum:

Attainment Target 4: Handling Data

Probability first occurs in the National Curriculum at Key Stage 2. It expects children to:

develop an understanding of probability,
through experience as well as experiment and theory,
and discuss events and simple experiments using vocabulary
that includes the words 'evens', 'fair', 'unfair', 'certain', 'likely', 'probably'.

Level 4 contains the first specific reference to probability and it expects children to understand and use the above vocabulary. Level 5 requires children to understand the probability scale from 0 to 1.

Activity:

The following pages include an explanation of how probability can be calculated in terms of chosen outcomes from a total of possible outcomes. Activities begin by looking at the number of possibilities when performing magic tricks, for example picking from a number of playing cards. The children are required to express probabilities as fractions, with the number on the bottom (the denominator) being the number of **possible** outcomes, and the number on top (the numerator) being the number of outcomes we wish to occur, or be **chosen**. These ideas are then linked with work covered in Book 3 to develop the notion of representing probabilities on a scale from 0 to 1.

Teaching points:

It is important for your child to have a pack of cards for the work that follows. Discuss the structure of the pack in terms of colours, suits, picture cards etc.

Emphasise the link between fractions and the probability scale.

Magic maths

Probability is all about finding out what chance there is of something happening.

1

Under one of these three cups is a coin. So we can say that there is a 'one out of three' chance you will pick the cup with the coin underneath. We can say this in different ways. It is a:

one out of three chance   **one in three chance**   **one-third chance**

And we write it like this:

probability of finding the coin = $\frac{1}{3}$

The probability of **not** finding the coin is 2 out of 3 chances, which we write as:

probability of not finding the coin = $\frac{2}{3}$

2

Here are six cards. Your friend is going to choose one without looking at them. Write the answers to these questions in the same way as the example above.

a What is the probability of your friend picking an ace from these cards?

....

b What is the probability of your friend picking a diamond from these cards?

....

c What is the probability of your friend picking a black card from these cards?

....

d What is the probability of your friend picking a jack from these cards?

....

e What is the probability of choosing a number less than 11?

....

52

3

Here is a full pack of cards. There are 52 cards in a pack, 4 suits and 13 cards in each suit.

Remember, there are always 52 possible cards to pick from!

a What is the probability of picking the ace of hearts? ......$\frac{1}{52}$......

b What is the probability of picking the ace of hearts or ace of clubs? ....

c What is the probability of picking any ace? ....

d What is the probability of picking a diamond? ....

e What is the probability of picking a picture card? (There are three in each suit.) ....

f What is the probability of picking the 9 of clubs? ....

g What is the probability of picking one of the cards on page 52 out of this pack? ....

h What is the probability of picking a red card? ....

4

Sometimes we are asked to show probability on a scale.

If you wanted to show a probability of $\frac{3}{8}$, then imagine the scale was split into 8 equal sections, then count 3 along and put a cross like this:

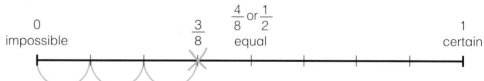

If you wanted to show a probability of $\frac{1}{52}$, you'd have to split the scale into 52 sections!

Now turn over ➤

Now try these ...

1   If you had a bag with 3 red beads, 5 blue beads and 2 yellow beads in it, what would
    be the probability of picking:

    a red bead?   ....   a blue bead?   ....

    a yellow bead?   ....   a white bead?   ....

    Can you mark the probability of picking each of these colours on this scale?

    0 $\frac{1}{2}$ 1

2   If you had a pencil case with 7 black pens, 6 orange pens, 3 brown pens and
    4 yellow pens in it, what would be the probability of picking:

    a brown pen?   ....   a yellow pen?   ....

    a black pen?   ....   an orange pen?   ....

    Can you mark the probability of picking each of these colours on this scale?

    0 $\frac{1}{2}$ 1

3   Stalybridge Celtic are a non-league football team who have got through to the third
    round of the FA Cup. There are 64 teams left in the competition, including:

    20 from the Premier League   17 from Division 1
    13 from Division 2   9 from Division 3
      4 other non-league teams

    What is the probability of Stalybridge Celtic being drawn to play against:

    a team from the Premier League? ....   a team from Division 1?   ....

    a team from Division 2?   ....   a team from Division 3?   ....

    a non-league team?   ....   Manchester United?   ....

More ways to help your child:

Discuss with your child things in everyday life that are based on probability, for example
weather forecasts, winning the lottery.

Practical activities with dice, collections of socks, coloured crayons etc. can provide
opportunities for questions such as, 'What is the probability of picking a blue sock?'

Duck shape
(page 25)

Angle measurer
(page 36)

Trace and copy
on to card. Cut
out and join the
two strips
together with a
paper fastener.

L shape
(page 8)

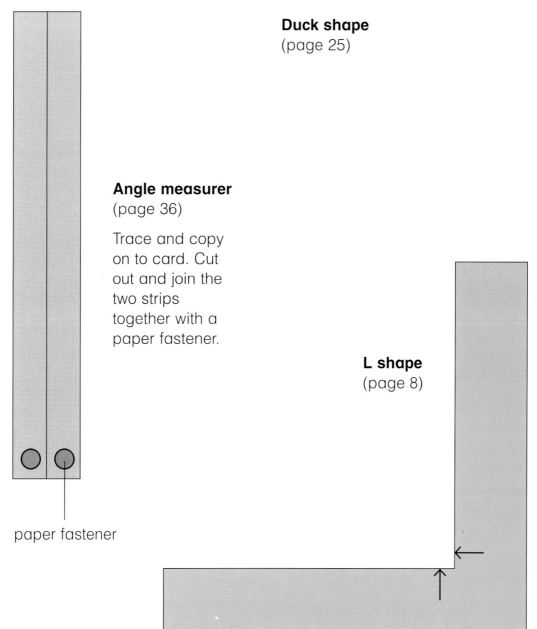

paper fastener

ANSWERS

Pages 4–5

1 a M 26390   T 26437   W 26499   Th 26548   F 26619
  b 47 miles

2 a 57 miles

4 Exact prices: a £13.02   b £9.07   c £15.35

Page 6

2   111   953   633   2869
    7683   16251   8171   6144

3 Exact prices: £7.37   £7.23   £11.63   £12.82   £6.59

Pages 8–9

1 25, 36, 49, 64, 81, 100

2 1, 2, 4, 8

3 **13** 13 × 1 prime
  9 3 × 3, 9 × 1 rectangular
  5 1 × 5 prime

Page 10

1 **square** 1, 4, 9, 16, 49, 64, 81
  prime 2, 3, 5, 7, 13, 71

2 **24** 1, 2, 3, 4, 6, 8, 12, 24   **29** 1, 29
  18 1, 2, 3, 6, 9, 18   **30** 1, 2, 3, 5, 6, 10, 15, 30
  36 1, 2, 3, 4, 6, 9, 12, 18, 36   **51** 1, 3, 17, 51
  48 1, 2, 3, 4, 6, 8, 12, 16, 24, 48 **64** 1, 2, 4, 8, 16, 32, 64

3   384   480   897   1462   6084   23424

Pages 12–13

2   6.5   30.8   92.4

5 a 9   b 7   c 5   d 13
   16p   4p   25p   25p

Page 14

1 a 8 cars   b 8 boxes   c 12 buses

2   10   11   10   11   11
    16   15   18   19   33

3   128.4   169.8   136.5   43.25   63.5

Pages 16–17

1 For example: 1 Big Ben and a milk or 1 burger and
  1 large fries

2   10   £19.90   £11.50   £8.80   4p   £39.80

3   £7.80   £4.50
    £9.20   £6.70
    10
    10

Page 18

1 a £3.10   d £3.50
  b £4.95   e £6.90
  c £7.15   f £13.40
  £20.25

2 a £6.90   e £7.42
  b £452.80   f £64,300
  c £140   g £3000
  d £750   h £1000

Pages 20–21

1   100   7   39   36   18

2   72   78   36

3   0.39   0.36   0.07

4   90   160   360

5 Fiona 60%   Pete 60%   Kevin 60%
  They all scored the same percentage.

Page 22

1 a   18   e   4
  b   6   f 200
  c   10   g 20
  d 150   h 30

2 a 50%   b 20%   c 25%

3 a 40%   b 20%   c 2%

4   80%   70%   90%
    79%   90%   80%
  Rachel and Joshua did the best, both scoring 90%

Page 24

2 a reflection   b reflection   c translation   d rotation
  e rotation   f translation

Page 26

1 translation 2 reflection 3 rotation 4 reflection 5 translation

Pages 28–29

1 b = 8   c = 8

3   Faces   Vertices   Edges
  a   6   8   12
  b   5   6   9
  c   6   5   9
  d   8   12   18
  e   5   5   8

Page 30

1 a 4   e 7   i 7
  b 11   f 7   j 14
  c 12   g 15   k 18
  d 15   h 38   l 20

2 x and y can equal all the numbers from 0 to 12,
  the two axes should be filled in with partners to 12.

3 F + V − E = 2
  F = E + 2 − V
  V = E + 2 − F

Pages 32–33

1 & 2 **length** ruler, tape measure, metre stick